anythink

D0700208

THE TOP SECRET LIFE OF PLANTS

HOW PLANTS PROTECT THEMSELVES

BY SARAH MACHAJEWSKI

Gareth Stevens
PUBLISHING

Please visit our website, www.garethstevens.com. For a free color catalog of all our high-quality books, call toll free 1-800-542-2595 or fax 1-877-542-2596.

Library of Congress Cataloging-in-Publication Data

Names: Machajewski, Sarah, author.
Title: How plants protect themselves / Sarah Machajewski.
Description: New York : Gareth Stevens Publishing, [2020] | Series: The top secret life of plants | Includes index.
Identifiers: LCCN 2018027862| ISBN 9781538233818 (library bound) | ISBN 9781538233795 (paperback) | ISBN 9781538233801 (6 pack)
Subjects: LCSH: Plant defenses–Juvenile literature. | Plants–Adaptation–Juvenile literature.
Classification: LCC QK921 .M33 2020 | DDC 581.4/7–dc23
LC record available at https://lccn.loc.gov/2018027862

First Edition

Published in 2020 by
Gareth Stevens Publishing
111 East 14th Street, Suite 349
New York, NY 10003

Designer: Sarah Liddell
Editor: Abby Badach Doyle

Photo credits: Cover, p. 1 (cactus) KIMZA/Shutterstock.com; glass dome shape used throughout bombybamby/Shutterstock.com; leaves used throughout janniwet/Shutterstock.com; background texture used throughout MInerva Studio/Shutterstock.com; p. 5 Ku-annuwar Sriraden/Shutterstock.com; p. 7 skynetphoto/Shutterstock.com; p. 9 thekovtun/Shutterstock.com; p. 11 patjo/Shutterstock.com; p. 13 (living stone plants) Rillke/Wikimedia Commons; p. 13 (*boquila trifoliata*) Oliv0/Wikimedia Commons; p. 15 Llez/Wikimedia Commons; p. 17 sutham/Shutterstock.com; p. 19 (roots) showcake/Shutterstock.com; p. 19 (stem) chinahbzyg/Shutterstock.com; p. 19 (leaves) Brian Tkalec/EyeEm/EyeEm/Getty Images; p. 19 (seed) Thanatham Piriyakarnjanakul/EyeEm/EyeEm/Getty images; p. 21 Robert Kneschke/Shutterstock.com.

Printed in the United States of America

CPSIA compliance information: Batch #CS19GS: For further information contact Gareth Stevens, New York, New York at 1-800-542-2595.

CONTENTS

Expert Survivors....4
The Secrets of Adaptations....6
Stay Back!....8
Protective Prickles....10
Hiding In Plain Sight....12
Deadly Plants....14
Shrinking from Danger....16
Plant Parts Are Protected....18
A Closer Look....20
Glossary....22
For More Information....23
Index....24

Words in the glossary appear in **bold** type the first time they are used in the text.

EXPERT SURVIVORS

When it comes to surviving in the wild, plants are very smart. Over time, plants have developed **savvy** ways of protecting themselves. But their **methods** aren't always easy to see.

Take a look at any of the plants that are around you. Are they really the quiet, gentle plants they appear to be, or are there hidden defenses at work? Let's uncover the top secret world of plant defenses.

CLASSIFIED!

A DEFENSE IS A FORM OF PROTECTION AGAINST AN ATTACK. STRONG DEFENSES ARE KEY TO A PLANT'S SURVIVAL.

THIS PLANT HAS A SUPERSECRET DEFENSE! CAN YOU GUESS WHAT IT IS? FIND OUT LATER IN THIS BOOK.

THE SECRETS OF ADAPTATIONS

There are thousands of plant **species** in the world, and all have perfected their defenses over time. Plants' unique, or special, ways of protecting themselves are called adaptations. An adaptation is a change that allows plants to better survive in their **environment**.

Adaptations are passed on to new plants over time, until the defense becomes part of the species. Some defenses, such as thorns, are easy to see. Others aren't as easy to see. But, they all play the same role: helping the plant survive.

CLASSIFIED!

JUST LIKE PLANTS, ANIMALS NEED PROTECTION. THEIR PROTECTIVE ADAPTATIONS INCLUDE SHARP CLAWS, POINTY TEETH, HARD SCALES, AND COLORING TO HELP THEM HIDE.

A THORN IS AN ADAPTATION THAT HELPS PROTECT PLANTS FROM PREDATORS THAT WANT TO TOUCH THEM OR EAT THEM.

STAY BACK!

Some plants are covered with tough thorns, sharp prickles, and pointy spines. Just the look of these plant parts tells predators to stay away!

The cactus uses spiky spines as its main defense. Cactus spines are actually a kind of leaf, and they do double duty as a form of protection. The spines prevent predators from touching or biting the plant, so it stays safe. When predators **encounter** the spines, they know to stay away. If they touch or try to eat the plant, they will get poked.

CLASSIFIED!

CACTUS SPINES ALSO PROTECT THE PLANT BY PROVIDING SHADE FROM THE STRONG DESERT SUN.

CACTUS SPINES COME IN MANY DIFFERENT SHAPES, SIZES, AND COLORS.

PROTECTIVE PRICKLES

Rose plants also **wield** a sharp defense. But you may not notice it at first. The plant's beautiful, sweet-smelling flower gets all the attention, and it **attracts** predators like hungry rabbits and deer. But if they get too close, they'll realize the plant is covered in sharp, pointy prickles. It's a clear warning: do not touch!

The sharp prickles keep predators from touching or eating the plant. This defense helps keep the flower safe, and the plant can continue to survive.

CLASSIFIED!

THE SECRET IS OUT: MANY PEOPLE THINK ROSES HAVE THORNS, BUT THEY ACTUALLY HAVE PRICKLES. PRICKLES ARE DIFFERENT THAN THORNS OR SPINES.

WHAT'S THE DIFFERENCE BETWEEN PRICKLES AND THORNS? PRICKLES BREAK OFF EASILY, BUT THORNS GROW FROM DEEPER IN THE PLANT'S STEM.

HIDING IN PLAIN SIGHT

Sometimes, a plant's best secret is knowing how to hide in plain sight! This type of defense is called camouflage (KAM-oh-flaw-zh). Camouflage is coloring that allows an **organism** to blend in with its surroundings.

Many plants use camouflage, but the *Lithops* (LIH-thawps) plant has a special top secret defense. These plants **disguise** themselves to look like dry stones in their desert habitat. Predators looking for plants to eat will walk right by without realizing it. Little do they know, these "stones" are really plants!

THE LIVING STONE PLANT COMES IN MANY COLORS. IT GROWS TWO BIG LEAVES THAT LOOK LIKE DESERT ROCKS.

living stone plants

CLASSIFIED!

THE *BOQUILA TRIFOLIOLATA* (BOH-*KEE*-LAH TRY-*FOH*-LEE-OH-*LAW*-TUH) VINE, FOUND IN THE RAIN FORESTS OF SOUTH AMERICA, CAN CHANGE THE WAY IT LOOKS TO MATCH WHATEVER PLANTS ARE NEARBY. IT CAN EVEN BLEND IN WITH TWO DIFFERENT PLANTS AT ONCE.

boquila trifoliolata vine

DEADLY PLANTS

Beautiful, sweet-smelling...and deadly? Some plants have poison that can make people and animals very sick...or worse. Poison is something you eat or drink that causes illness or death. Plants that protect themselves with poison include deadly nightshade, castor bean, white snakeroot, and lily of the valley.

A plant's poison can be very powerful. Eating or simply touching a poisonous plant can have very serious **consequences**. Poison sends a clear message to predators: stay away, or else.

CLASSIFIED!

THROUGHOUT HISTORY, POISONOUS PLANTS WERE USED AS MURDER **WEAPONS**! SOCRATES, AN IMPORTANT THINKER IN ANCIENT TIMES, WAS POISONED BY WATER HEMLOCK.

THIS BEAUTIFUL BELLADONNA PLANT, OR DEADLY NIGHTSHADE, LOOKS HARMLESS...BUT YOU CAN'T SEE THE POISON HIDDEN INSIDE THE PLANT'S CELLS!

SHRINKING FROM DANGER

When you feel scared, do you ever want to run away and hide? Plants can't protect themselves like that, so they use other defenses. The *Mimosa pudica* (mih-MOH-suh POO-dih-kuh), known as the **sensitive** plant, has a very surprising secret: it can move!

When a predator brushes up against the sensitive plant, it quickly closes its leaves. When its leaves fold shut, the plant no longer looks like a tasty meal. The rapid movement may surprise predators, too. The leaves reopen within a few minutes, long after the predator has gone.

HOW DOES IT MOVE? WHEN THE *MIMOSA PUDICA* IS TOUCHED, WATER DRAINS FROM CELLS AT THE BASE OF ITS *LEAVES*, CAUSING THEM TO CLOSE.

PLANT PARTS ARE PROTECTED

Most plants are made up of the same basic parts. Each part has a job to help the plant survive. That's why each part has to be protected in a special way.

A seed has a tiny plant inside of it. It's protected by a hard outer shell, called a seed coat. Roots are hidden underground, where layers of soil protect them from our feet. Stems stay strong by a thick outer wrapper, kind of like human skin. Leaves have a waxy coating that protects them from damage.

PLANTS HAVE ADAPTED OVER TIME TO PROTECT EACH PART OF THEIR "BODIES." IT'S NO SECRET: PLANTS ARE REALLY GOOD AT DEFENSE!

PROTECT EVERY PART!

ROOTS

hidden underground

STEMS

tough, skin-like covering

LEAVES

covered in a waxy coating to keep water in and protect against hungry bugs

SEEDS

surrounded by a hard shell to protect the tiny plant inside

A CLOSER LOOK

Plants may seem peaceful and still. But now you know they're preparing for top secret battles, right under your nose! Whether it has prickles, poison, or camouflage, a plant's defenses are some of its best-kept secrets. Smart defenses are how plants protect themselves, keep predators away, and survive to see another day.

What other kinds of plant protections are out in the natural world? Take a closer look at the plants you see around you. Can you spy any supersecret defenses at work?

WHAT SECRETS DOES THIS PLANT HAVE TO TELL?

GLOSSARY

attract: to draw nearer

consequence: an outcome or result

disguise: the state of having a false appearance

encounter: to come across

environment: the natural world in which a plant or animal lives

method: a way of doing something

organism: a living thing

savvy: smart, clever

sensitive: able to sense or feel changes in surroundings

species: a group of plants or animals that are all of the same kind

weapon: something used to cause injury or death

wield: to have something and be ready to use it

FOR MORE INFORMATION

BOOKS

Belvins, Wiley. *Ninja Plants: Survival and Adaptation in the Plant World.* Minneapolis, MN: Twenty-First Century Books, 2017.

Leedy, Loreen. *Amazing Plant Powers: How Plants Fly, Fight, Hide, Hunt and Change the World.* New York, NY: Holiday House, 2015.

Owen, Ruth. *How Do Plants Defend Themselves?* New York, NY: PowerKids Press, 2015.

WEBSITES

DK Find Out: All About Plants!
www.dkfindout.com/us/animals-and-nature/plants/
Explore the wild world of plants, including their fascinating defenses.

Science for Kids: Plant Defenses
www.scienceforkidsclub.com/plant-defenses.html
Learn how plants defend and protect themselves against predators.

Science Kids: Plants for Kidss
www.sciencekids.co.nz/plants.html
Take quizzes, watch videos, and play games to learn fun facts about plants.

INDEX

adaptation 6, 7
belladonna 15
boquila trifoliolata 13
camouflage 12, 20
cactus 8, 9
cactus spines 8, 9
castor bean 14
defense 4, 6, 10, 12, 16, 20
habitat 12, 18
lily of the valley 14
Lithops 12
living stone plant 13
Mimosa pudica 16
nightshade 14
plant parts 19
poison 14, 20
prickles 8, 10, 11, 20
rose 10, 11
Socrates 14
thorns 6, 7, 8, 11
water hemlock 14
white snakeroot 14